A Word, Shared

FAITH-FILLED POEMS TO ENCOURAGE AND INSPIRE

"Like a sunflower seeking out the light,
I turn my face towards your sight."

Elizabeth Rushmer

A Heard Word, Shared
by Elizabeth Rushmer

First published 2020

Copyright © Elizabeth Rushmer 2020

Book interior by Eleanor Abraham.
Cover design by Mark Mechan of Red Axe Design.
Cover image: Phil Taylor Photography.

Interior illustrations by ilonita, aksol and Ekonst,
courtesy of Shutterstock.
Typeset in Bodoni URW.

Contents

Loved	7
Chosen	8
Found	9
Restore Me	10
No Hope	11
Freed	12
Take My Hand	13
My Child	14
I Hear You	15
My Hope	16
Rescued	17
Come	18
Watching	19
Alone	20
Hold Me	21
Reveal Yourself	22
Fragile	23
Chains	24
Rebuilt	25
Brave	26
Cleaning	27
Enter	28
Praying	29
Window	30
Sunflower	31
Try	32
Faith	33
Enemy	34
Follow	36
He Knows	37
Let Go	38

Leaning   39
Too Heavy   40
Gripped   41
Lifted   42
Special   43
Struggling   44
Promises   45
Reaping   46
Pause   47
Calling   48
Go Tell   49
Proclaim   50
Need   51
Beside You   52
Beacon   53
Problem   54
Lasting   55
Changing   56
Purpose   57
Fog   58
Mistake   59
Fighting   60
Stand Out   61
I See You   62
Love Given   63
Strengthen Me   64
Each Day   65
Show Me   66
Revive Us   67
Time Together   68
Come Again   70
Lead Me   71
Use Me   72
Fortify Me   73
Price Paid   74

Harder	75
Repent	76
My Place	77
Your Love	78
Know Him	79
Comfort	80
Blinkered	81
Carry You	82
Whispers	83
Joy	84
Foundation	85
Seek Him	86
Gift	87
Cling On	88
Complete	89
Battle	90
Stand Firm	91
Focus	92
Side By Side	93
Recharge	94
Step Out	95
Peace	96
Hope	97
Distractions	98
Faults	99
Throne	100
Weeping	101
Remember	102
Boldness	103
Troubles	104
Rainbow	105
Light	106
Sing	107
Change	108
Call Out	109

Through You   110
Tending   111
Walking   112
Fun   113
No Fear   114
In the Gap   115
Tune In   116
Open Heart   117
Example   118
Signpost   119
Flow   120
My All   121
Words   122
Draw Me In   123
Untidy   124
Replay   125
Beat   126
Break   127
Counted   128
Think   129
Prepare me   130
Willing   131
Washed   132
Adapt   133
Bubble   134
Escape   135
Retreat   136
Why?   138
Magic   139
Comments   140
Future   141
Birdsong   142
Stir Us   143

Loved

You are special to me,
it's you I love the most.
You mean everything to me,
I want to keep you close.
Though you may not feel it,
please believe it's true —
I sent my son down to earth
to give his life for you.
So don't say that you're nothing
or your life is not worth living,
I have given it to you
and I want to keep on giving.

Chosen

He chose you,
he knew you from the start,
he's seen how you live your life,
he knows what's in your heart.
He chose you,
you don't have to be the best,
demonstrate useful skills
or pass a final test.
He chose you,
you don't need to be well
  dressed,
have lots of money in the bank
or offer more than all the rest.
He chose you.

Found

I was hiding but you knew where to find me.
I was blinkered but you took them so I'd see.
I was damaged but you bandaged me up.
I was lacking but now I know I'm enough.
I was deaf but you ensured the message got
  through.
I was alone but now I have you.

Restore Me

Restore me, Lord, from what I was,
make me whole again.
Wipe my tears and heal my hurts,
break the bondage chain.
I did not know I needed you
but I can't manage on my own.
I walk along the path I chose,
but if only I had known
that going this way would bring
   despair
and death would come to me.
But in you there is life and love
and all goodness comes from thee.

No Hope

I'm stuck in a pit of anger and despair,
some hear me call out but they don't care,
others try to help but they just can't reach.
I'm too far gone, I'm in too deep.
It's dark and lonely, I cannot cope,
there's no way out, I've lost all hope.
But you hear me cry and you come to save,
you lift me out of my self-made grave,
you tend my wounds and you clean me up,
you let me drink from your life-giving cup.
I am now made righteous in Jesus' name.
My burden is lifted, you've taken my
    shame.

Freed

Heal the pain that's gripping my soul,
remove the many chains tied on to me.
I'm burdened and weighed down by my
  mistakes,
I can't take it — I want to be free.
I've followed the wrong path seeking
  release
but worldly ways can't provide what I
  need.
I'm a broken person — I can't heal myself
so I turn to Jesus so that I can be freed.

Take My Hand

Take my hand, Lord, it's too dark to see,
lead me back to where I ought to be.
I've strayed and the path is far from sight.
I've grown too weary and lost my fight.
I need to be rescued, refreshed, made new,
the only hope I have is you.
Forgive me, Lord, help me start again,
cleanse my heart and release my pain.
Wipe my tears so I can clearly see
I'm not alone because you're with me.
My choices, Lord, have made this space,
and you wait for me to accept your grace.
Your unfailing love will set me free,
I accept your gracious gift to me.

My Child

Don't doubt your importance to me
I've loved you from the start.
I knew you at the beginning,
you are always on my heart.
I know life hasn't always been easy,
and I know the tears you've cried,
but you're my child and I love you
and I've never left your side.

I Hear You

I hear you calling out to me
and I must answer you.
You pursued my hardening heart,
softened it, made it new.
I no longer feel alone,
and my hurts begin to mend
knowing that you're by my side,
my saviour, Lord and friend.
Redeeming, healing, teaching me,
you point the way to go;
you plant your love within my life
encouraging it to grow.
You don't demand a perfect being,
just a willing open heart.
You will take me as I am,
I simply have to start.
There's so much that I don't know,
a great deal I don't understand,
but I just need to trust in you
and seek your guiding hand.

My Hope

Break the bonds that hold me captive,
bring the freedom I desperately need.
Release me from unmanageable
    burdens,
whatever it takes, I long to be freed.
You alone can bring redemption,
the only hope I have is you.
Break these chains then I'm yours
    forever,
and I'll live the life you ask me to.

Rescued

You've rescued me, Lord,
my life's no longer the same.
I've been redeemed and made
    righteous
in Jesus' name.
The veil has been lifted,
I now clearly see
the wonderful gift
freely given to me.
I'm accepted and loved,
I've been welcomed in,
my past is forgiven,
I've been cleansed of my sin.
I'm a child of God,
a creation made new,
I am free, made complete,
and treasured by you.

Come

You know me and you love me
regardless of what I've done.
When I shy away in the darkness
you call on me to come,
come to you, to speak with you,
to share my hurts with you.
Only you can heal me
and that's what you want to do.

Watching

You see me struggling with my burdens;
time after time, I falter and fall,
weighed down with the pressure of wrong
    choices.
I just can't manage to handle it all.
The offer's there, you want to help me,
I just have to accept it and take your
    hand,
you easily lift it and remove it from me,
no longer burdened I'm free to stand.

Alone

Comfort me in the silence
when there's no one else around.
Lift me out of the darkness
when all I want to do is go to ground.
Soothe away my stresses
so my head can clearly think.
Anchor me to your steadfast rock
so in the waves I will not sink.

Hold Me

Scoop me up and hold me tight
I've lost the will to stand and fight.
Reason and logic no longer hold,
I can't make sense of all I've been
    told.
I have no answers, nothing seems
    clear,
I've lost my smile and all my cheer.
All I can do is sit and pray
and look to you to guide my way.

Reveal Yourself

Please reveal yourself to me,
open my eyes so I can see,
open my heart so I understand,
open my mind to what you have planned.
I want to walk in step with you,
be obedient to what you'll have me do.
Guide me through all the days I live,
I'm open to all you have to give.

Fragile

Please take care of my heart, it's fragile,
it's broken and full of pain.
Please hold it together in your hands
and help me to love again.
At the moment I don't see a way through
    this,
all there is is confusion and fear.
But I'm trusting in you to carry me,
to lift me up and keep me near.

Chains

Break the chains that hold me
    down
and set me free to run.
Wipe the slate of all past wrongs,
forget the bad I've done.
I regret it all, and turn to you
to start afresh today.
I turn my back on what I was.
I choose a better way.

Rebuilt

Like a broken piece of pottery,
I was shattered to the core.
I couldn't see a future,
I couldn't hope for more.
But you found me and you saved
    me,
rebuilt me, made me new.
Your love has fully changed me;
anything is possible because of you.

Brave

Make me brave to face the day
and all unknown things to come.
Give me strength to take a stand,
to not give up and run.
Help me speak out for what is just,
to not be intimidated by the strong.
Impart your wisdom to me
so I'll always know right from
   wrong.

Cleaning

You're filing down the rough edges,
scrubbing away anything unclean,
polishing me up slowly,
so something beautiful can be
    seen.
I'm impatient for transformation
but it's a job that can't be rushed,
I know I won't ever be perfect
but I will always be enough.

Enter

Come to me, my children,
my arms are open wide.
Enter into my embrace
and in my safety hide.
You can't control things around
    you,
I know it's all too much to bear,
so speak to me of your problems
and I'll meet your needs with
    care.

Praying

I'm praying for you in this time of
    trouble,
there's not much else I can do.
I don't have any answers
but the Lord will see you through.
He knows you and he loves you,
he's with you through this time.
He'll strengthen you for the journey
and take your hand for the uphill
    climb.

Window

Open a window into my heart,
breathe your breath into me,
remove the scales from in front of my eyes
so I can finally see.
Lift off my burdens and lighten my load,
release all that I no longer require,
refocus my mind simply on you,
ignite my passion for what you desire.

Sunflower

Like a sunflower seeking out the light,
I turn my face towards your sight.
Your radiance and glory warms me through,
I've thrown off the old and been made new.
You replenish me with your strength and
    power,
you're by my side each and every hour.
You give me courage to face the day,
strengthen my faith so I'll never turn away.
It won't be easy and I'll feel life's stress
but only in you will I find my ultimate rest.

Try

Yesterday I could handle this,
I felt confident, able and strong,
but today just isn't working out
it feels like everything I do is
    wrong.
But I mustn't let it get me down
even if there's fear and pain,
so when tomorrow comes around
I'm going to get up and try again.

Faith

I can't be parted from your love
no matter what befalls me.
Regardless of the things around,
I know you're fighting for me.
You just need me to keep the faith
and stand firm upon your word,
to praise you in the hard times,
and know my prayers are heard.

Enemy

The enemy whispers his lies in my ear,
not very loud, but always quite clear,
building on doubts and poking at pain,
reminding of errors and moments of shame.
It's hard to distinguish his voice from my stuff
but I've had it with him, enough is enough!
I'm taking a stand and I'll accept it no more,
I'm building a wall and locking the door.
In future it's only God's word that's accepted,
I'm loved as I am and never rejected.
I've welcomed my saviour so now I am free,
I can move forward with life, be who God wants
    me to be.
It's a continuous battle, I'm going to need help,
it's not always easy accepting yourself.

I'd never say to any friend of mine,
"You're no good at that, you're wasting your
    time,
there's no point in struggling, you can't be your
    best,
you're not that important, you're not as good as
    the rest."
And if I wouldn't speak to another this way,
when the thoughts are about me, why let them
    stay?
So the moment it starts, I'm taking a stand,
remembering I'm a child of God, yes I am.

Follow

You call me out to walk with you,
to follow where you lead.
I may not have what it takes
but you'll give me what I need.
I may not fully understand
the plan you have for me,
but I know that I should trust
and believe, even when I don't see.

He Knows

God knows what you've been going
    through,
he's been with you all the way,
and now he's brought you out of it,
he'll make you stronger every day.
He'll restore what once was lost
and make it up to you,
so that in your coming days
you can praise him in all you do.
Don't take this life for granted,
it was given as a gift.
The God of heaven loves you
but it's time to make a switch.
Focus your eyes on heaven
and come to know the Lord,
immerse yourself in his kindness
and become familiar with his word.
He's saved you for a purpose,
he has a job for you to do,
so listen for his whispers
as he guides and leads you through.

Let Go

Don't feel ashamed of the tears you cry
or the anxiety that flows through you.
It's only natural to feel this way,
but it's not something to hold on to.
Put your trust in one who's bigger than this,
who always remains the same,
in him you'll find peace, love and joy
and Jesus is his name.

Leaning

Strip away my fear and pain,
bandage me up, make me whole again,
keep me strong when the doubts creep in,
hold me close when the troubles begin.
Left alone I won't get through,
but I can do all things if I lean on you.

Too Heavy

It lightens my heart
to give my burdens to you,
they're too heavy to carry
there's no more I can do.
You alone are strong enough
to deal with it all.
You kept on offering
but I was deaf to your call.
How foolish it seems
to try to cope on my own,
as you're at my side
so I'm never alone.
I'm going to loosen my grip
and let it all go,
so the peace that you give
I'll fully know.

Gripped

Gripped by the fear and darkness,
I can't claw my own way out.
There's no one around to help me,
no ear to hear my shout.
But through the heavy silence,
as my heart screams out in pain,
you are there to rescue me, Lord,
lift me up, make me whole again.

Lifted

Be lifted up by the one who loves you,
don't dwell in anxiety and fear,
turn to the Lord with a humble heart
and let him draw you near.
Put your trust in him who understands
and knows the things you face.
He'll pour out his loving kindness upon you,
his blessings and his grace.

Special

Don't struggle alone, lean into me,
I am everything you need me to be.
Just focus your mind on the task at hand,
and I'll be with you as you follow my
    plan.
Times will be hard but there is a way
    through,
you are my child and I dearly love you.
I won't let you down, I'm holding you
    close,
you're special to me, I love you the most.

Struggling

Lord help me to let go
and put my trust in you,
I'm anxious and scared
and not sure what to do.
All of my life
I've kept to a plan,
now everything's changing,
it's getting out of hand.
I'm not sure what'll happen
from one day to the next,
living with uncertainty
is not what I do best.
But one thing I'm sure of
is that you're always the same,
and in you I find refuge
until life's normal again.

Promises

Silence the voices inside your head,
the ones that are speaking out fears.
It is not your destiny to live this way,
I've planned joy for you, not sorrow and
   tears.
Hold on to the promises that I've given,
repeat them and speak them out loud,
for through you I will accomplish great
   things,
I want you to work towards what I have
   planned.

Reaping

You need to call out to me,
you can't manage on your own.
You must ask for forgiveness,
you're reaping what you've sown.
Selfishness and greed
are not what I desire.
Don't look to man for your morals,
you must lift your eyes up higher.
The rules that I have given
are because of my love for you.
I want you to be happy,
so I've shown you what to do.
Please don't ignore me any longer
now is the time to repent,
let me direct you in the way
your life can be better spent.

Pause

Just pause a moment and sit a while,
take some time to think of me.
There's no need to keep on rushing,
stop your doing and try just to be.
Clear your mind of all your worries,
give them up for me to hold.
Just be still and know I'm God,
open your heart to the truth I hold.

Calling

I know you and I love you
but you need to heed my call.
No longer fulfilling your own desires,
you must give me your all.
You can only go so far in life
if you choose to please yourself,
so turn to me, discover your worth,
lean on me, I'm here to help.

Go Tell

Lead all others to me,
they must be told about me.
They must have their eyes opened,
and given the chance to see.
You can't keep it to yourself,
my truth's too good not to share,
it's your job to go and tell them
and to show them that you care.

Proclaim

Speak it and live it,
proclaim my good news.
People must hear it
before they can choose.
How will they find life
if they're not given a choice?
Lead them to me,
and hear heaven rejoice.

Need

I'm calling out to you —
all those who have ignored me before.
I want you to come to me,
it's what I am longing for.
For too long you've done things your way
but you must realise you need me now.
I can turn your life around,
come to me and I'll show you how.

Beside You

You're not on your own,
though you may feel that way,
I am beside you
and I am here to stay.
Tell me your troubles
and I'll give you my peace.
Pour out your heartache
and I'll give you release.
Come into my arms,
you can find solace there.
When you rely on me
I'll meet your every need and care.

Beacon

When I'm lost and all alone,
you're the beacon I keep in sight.
When darkness is surrounding me,
you are my guiding light.
You offer your hand to me
when I struggle to find my way,
you share your wisdom with me
when I don't know what to say.
Without you there's something missing,
I could never be complete,
so I praise you for all that you are
as I worship at your feet.

Problem

I don't have to have all the answers,
the problem's too big for me.
I don't understand all the angles,
the bigger picture's too hard to see.
I've tried and failed to grasp it,
so instead I'm giving it to you,
you're the only one who can sort it,
and I'll trust in what you do.

Lasting

Where do I find my joy?
Is it in something that will last?
Do I look for happiness and fulfilment
in something that's gone too fast?
I want something that lasts forever,
that I can always hold on to,
something that will bring me love and
    peace.
God, I place my hope in you.

Changing

Under the makeup and social veneer,
you can't see the anxiety, I'm hiding the fear.
I've put on my mask to cope with the day,
I've perfected my smile and the right words to
    say.
I'm scared of rejection, that I don't really fit in,
I can't let people get close and see what's
    within.
I don't know who I am because I'm never the
    same,
I adapt to fit in, a shape-shifting game.
But why should their way be the correct way to
    be?
Perhaps it's time to stop and find the real me.

Purpose

You were created for a purpose
and to be completely you.
There are challenges and tasks in life
that only you can do.
You were formed to be unique –
fearfully and wonderfully made –
so look within, search yourself,
discover the gifts God gave.
Develop your skills and share your
    talents,
have courage, stand apart from the rest.
Have confidence in who you are,
so that others may be blessed.

Fog

You don't want me to stay in this fog of
  self pity,
with angry thoughts churning round in
  my head.
'Please don't dwell on them,' I hear you
  say,
'just give it all up to me instead.'
The enemy wants to keep me in worry,
to stay in a pit of despair,
but God is there to grab my hand,
rescue me and pull me up for air.

Mistake

A mistake doesn't make me a failure,
I just wasn't at my best that day.
A bad choice doesn't mean that all is lost,
I just took a wrong turn along the way.
Each day is made up of many decisions,
there is always so much going on.
I need to be loving and forgive myself
and value lessons learnt from things gone
    wrong.

Fighting

I keep thinking I'm progressing
and then I get set back,
the enemy knows my weakness
and he's always on the attack.
It's too easy to get downhearted
and think that all is lost,
but I'll continue to fight against it
and follow Jesus whatever the cost.

Stand Out

I don't have to play by the world's rules
    anymore,
I no longer need to fit in.
It's my job to stand out for Jesus,
he bought my life when he paid for my sin.
My life is his, so I'll follow where he leads,
I'll keep listening to every word.
I won't be conformed to the ways of this world,
but speak out until everyone has heard.

I See You

I sense you in creation,
in the vastness of the skies.
I see you in the gracefulness
of the bird that swoops and flies.
I see your hand in the detail
of even the smallest living thing.
I feel you in the sun and wind,
in the warmth and cooling that
    they bring.
I wonder at your creativity
as I view varieties of plants and
    trees —
all the evidence points towards you
so how could I not believe?

Love Given

Help me to love
with a love that's bigger than me.
Help me to see beyond
and recognise what it is you see.
Help me to not expect
anything in return for what I do,
but help me to be satisfied
that my reward will come from you.
Let my love go further
than a simple earthly love,
and help me to demonstrate
that which is given from above.

Strengthen Me

Strengthen me for this fight,
defend me against the enemy.
Protect me from the pain and hurt,
place your loving arms around me.
Help me stay in a place of peace,
fill me with your joy and love.
Let me not be dragged down to the depths,
but keep my eyes fixed on what's above.

Each Day

Use each of your days wisely,
take a moment to reassess
what is it that's important to you —
are there things you should stop or do
    less?
Reconnect with any loved ones
you were previously too busy for.
Spend more time with your family,
instead of always rushing out the door.
Enjoy the simple pleasures
of chatting and having fun.
Try to take a break from busyness
and worrying about what needs to be
    done.

Show Me

Give me a vision of how things should be,
show me a picture of where to go now.
We know there's so much wrong with our world —
it needs fixing but it's not quite clear how.
So many complex problems exist,
how can I possibly make a difference today?
But every journey starts with one step,
so please show me what part I can play.
If we all come together and do what we can,
show our care and concern for each other,
then surely the love would begin to pour out,
and the world could start to heal and recover.

Revive Us

Sweep through this land
and set hearts on fire.
Revive our souls
with your one desire:
to know you and to love you,
to praise your holy name,
to unite together in worship,
until you come again.

Time Together

It should be all about you, Lord,
but it's easy to get lost
and caught up in our doing,
but it's done at a cost.
Help me to remember
you want time just with me,
to sit quietly together,
to talk and just be.
It's the praise and the worship,
the love in my heart,
that means so much more
than me playing my part.

Good works grow from faith
but they're not enough on their own,
it's the time spent with you, Lord
where my faith will be grown.
My worth isn't found
in all the tasks that I do
but in knowing I'm chosen
and loved completely by you.
I have Christ's faith
and his spirit in me.
I am complete in Christ Jesus
and now totally free.

Come Again

Come on the clouds and revisit the earth,
there's so much that needs to be put right.
I don't know how much longer we must wait,
but I look forward to that glorious sight.
We know our limitations, our hope is in you,
teach us to be effective in our time.
Help us to live how you want us to live
so we'll hear you say, 'These people are mine'.

Lead Me

Help me walk the path you set,
lead me the right way.
If left alone, I'll wander off,
I need your help each day.
I can't be trusted all alone,
to say or do the right thing.
I need the love and wisdom,
that only you can bring.

Use Me

Speak to me the words you have
that others need to hear.
Show me what you want to say
so I can make it clear.
Use me, Lord, to spread your word,
to help draw others near,
so they can see your love for them
and no longer need to fear.

Fortify Me

You fortify me with your love,
you build me up inside.
I know I can rely on you
to be my strength and guide.
Sometimes the world just makes no
    sense –
I can't always find my way.
But with you at my side I know
I'll make it through the day.

Price Paid

I wasn't worthy of your life
but you paid the price for me,
you quietly took my punishment
and were nailed upon that tree.
But death was not the end for you,
it could not keep you there,
you've risen up to reign over us,
leaving the world your love to
   share.

Harder

Sometimes I feel like I'm just not enough
though I know I couldn't be much more.
Sometimes I know I have to go in,
but I just don't want to walk through the door.
Sometimes I have to fix a smile on my face
when I'm just not feeling it inside.
Sometimes I have to admit it won't work
despite how hard I have tried.
Sometimes it all seems much more difficult,
though I really couldn't explain why.
Sometimes I don't want to take part in the day,
but regardless I always will try.

Repent

Remove the past in one fell swoop,
just come to me today.
Repent of sins, give them to me.
I'll always listen when you pray.
The time is now, it's not too late,
you can be redeemed to me.
Give up the past and let it go,
be all you were meant to be.

My Place

I no longer need to run away,
you've shown me where I belong.
You are patient and loving to me,
you forgive me when I'm wrong.
If I come and say I'm sorry,
you welcome me to your side.
I know that I have found my place
and I never have to hide.

Your Love

Lord let your love flow through me,
my own supply is running short.
I do the things I shouldn't
and I don't do what I ought.
Help me be an example
of selfless love to all,
create in me a willingness
to respond to those that call.
Help me be receptive
even if the timing isn't great.
Help me be compassionate
when I'm tired and it's getting late.
Create in me forgiveness
to let the wrongs of others go.
Remove all selfishness within
so that it's your love that's on show.

Know Him

It isn't a secret that's hidden,
it's plain for all to see
that the God of earth and heaven
is in love with you and me.
He wants you to come to know him
and accept his love today,
search your heart, and answer his call,
and he'll help you find your way.

Comfort

The Lord sees and knows your troubles,
he's with you all the way,
he's there to comfort and guide you,
to help you through the day.
So turn to him and seek his help,
take comfort from his words,
he loves you more than you can know,
he's there to heal your hurts.

Blinkered

Lord remove the blinkers so I can clearly see.
Reveal my faults that are hidden to me.
Help me change and correct my ways
so I can walk in love the rest of my days.

Carry You

Focus your eyes upon the Lord,
when there's chaos all around.
Submerge yourself within his word,
let his love for you abound.
Proclaim his promises, trust in him,
he'll shine light to guide your way.
And when you're feeling tired and lost,
know that he will carry you that day.

Whispers

Please attune my ear, Lord
to the whisper of your word.
Let none of your prompts
be ignored or go unheard.
Make me more attentive
to the quiet requests you bring.
Help me be responsive,
to even the smallest thing.
Teach me to be obedient
through the challenges of each day.
Draw me closer to you
and align me with your way.

Joy

I'm going to tune out the voices of
    discontent
and focus on joy today.
They're trying to get us all stirred up
but we don't have to respond that way.
There are injustices that must be fought,
but there are some things we should let
    go.
Don't be dragged into anger and hate,
instead let your love overflow.

84

Foundation

What are you building your life upon?
Is your foundation steady and strong?
What do you have to cling to
if everything starts to go wrong?
Be sure to put your faith in something
that can support you when times are
    tough.
If you build your life around money and
    pleasure
that's not going to be enough.

Seek Him

Live your life as God desires,
listen out for his commands.
You're on earth to live his way,
he's not there to meet your
    demands.
Open your heart and learn his ways,
take time to seek his face.
Humble yourself before his throne
and be welcomed into his embrace.

Gift

Thank you, Lord Jesus,
for what you did for me,
you were nailed to the cross
so I'd be set free.
Your pain and your suffering
I can hardly believe,
but your gift, freely given,
I gratefully receive.

Cling On

In times of darkness and days of sorrow
fix your eyes upon me,
I will give you the strength and words
for all you need to be.
Give me your pain and all your anguish
and I will give you rest,
let go of things you can't control
and, through you, others will be blessed.
It won't be easy, and times are hard,
but your faith will see you through.
Cling on to me in all your worries
and I will help in all you do.

Complete

You've lived your life all this time
just trying to please yourself,
chasing happiness through different things,
status, fun and wealth.
But there's just one treasure you should seek
to fill the void within,
that's a relationship with the one true God,
you're only made complete in him.

Battle

The darkness is coming,
I can feel it closing in,
it's time to do battle,
though it's already written who will
    win.
I won't focus on the trouble
but lift my eyes up above.
The enemy cannot win this,
the victor will be love.

Stand Firm

I will stand firm in these testing times
and hold on to the promises you give.
I will read and speak your truth,
it's by your love I want to live.
So fill me with your spirit,
and make your home in me.
Help me live a life that's right
so I can be who I ought to be.

Focus

I could fear an unknown future,
I could worry about what lies ahead,
I could live in a state of anxiety
with only negativity in my head.
But, instead, I choose to focus
on all the love and joy around.
I put my trust and hope in the one
where grace and favour are to be found.

Side By Side

Stand with me in all I'm facing,
stay with me right by my side,
and if I can't take it any longer
in your arms I know I can hide.
Alone I'm not strong enough for battle,
and it's inevitable I'll face tough times,
but I look forward to walking with you
to seeing your miracles, wonders and
     signs.

Recharge

Where can I plug myself in,
I need to recharge my battery,
I've given my all to everyone else
I've nothing left for me.
It's not that I don't want to
be useful, helpful and kind,
but if I can't have some moments alone
I won't find rest for my body and mind.
I've had to learn what it is I need,
and I know I can only be at my best
if I take time to shut the world out
and find a place of quiet and rest.

Step Out

I need to start stepping out
and living by my faith.
I give my all to the Lord —
can't stop and play it safe.
His plans for me I do not know
but I'll follow where he leads.
My strength's in him, he's got my trust,
he knows and meets my needs.
It's my job to be a light
and share his love with all,
to grow in faith, become more like Christ,
and be obedient to his call.

Peace

Still my mind and let me find peace
beyond the struggles of the day.
There are so many choices and decisions to
    make
that it's hard to find the right way.
The noise outside seems too much to bear,
I need to shut it out.
I need peace and quiet and time to think,
to understand what it's all about.
I don't want any more information,
in fact, I think I'd be better with less.
There is just too much going on –
all my thoughts are in a mess.
So I'm stopping right now to take a break.
I no longer know what to say.
There's only one solution at a time like this,
to get on my knees and pray.

Hope

I've failed you again. I had such high hopes –
I should have learnt my lesson by this time.
I understood what my problem was,
so figured from now on I'd be fine.
But, yet again, I repeat my mistakes,
I'm not even sure where I went wrong.
I need your help, I can't change myself,
I try my best but I'm just not that strong.
But I don't need to panic, in you I find hope,
and on you I can place all my trust,
The choice is mine whether I accept your love,
and in my heart I know that I must.

Distractions

So many voices shouting
but it's your whisper I long to hear.
I push all other noise away –
it's only you that I want near.
Only you offer life and truth,
only you want the best for me.
All other distractions will hold me back,
but only you can set me free.

Faults

You slowly reveal to me
where I'm going wrong
but not too much at once,
you know I'm not that strong.
You don't leave me on my own
to figure out what I should do,
you teach me and guide me
and ask me to lean on you.

Throne

It's hard to believe the gift freely given,
you were crucified for me but now you are
   risen.
No longer entombed in the dark all alone,
you've taken your place, you sit on your throne.
You wait for us there to welcome us in,
you want everyone to enter, to turn from their
   sin.
It's easy to do, he's done the hard part,
you need to ask for forgiveness and humble
   your heart.
Turn your back on what was, then, watch your
   life renew.
Open your heart, he's calling to you.

Weeping

You call out to me in the darkness
when I should be fast asleep.
You want me to tell your people
to listen to you weep.
You're saddened by the situation
that we find ourselves in.
We must turn our eyes towards you
and turn our backs upon our sin.

Remember

Heavenly Father I ask and I pray
that you fill me right up with your love every
    day.
I start each day afresh and anew,
there's hope in my heart as my eyes turn to
    you.
But as the minutes and hours keep on
    ticking by,
I forget my plan and I don't even try.
I'm on automatic as I tick off each task,
your desire for me I don't remember to ask.
So help me to focus on how you want me to
    live,
show me opportunities where my help I can
    give.
Help me remember it's not all about me,
and let me view others in the way that you
    see.
I want to shine brightly for you every day,
I just need you to keep on showing me the
    way.

Boldness

The time is upon us for boldness,
to speak of what you believe.
If you don't proclaim the good
    news
how can others hear and receive?
Don't keep this precious gift quiet,
it's meant to be given to all,
you must be brave and share it
so everyone can answer God's call.

Troubles

Don't absorb the troubles of the day,
you'll only feel helpless and weighed down this
    way.
Instead, lift them up to God with praise
and he'll remove the tension of your days.
He loves you more than you can know,
and wants to show you the way to go.
Don't be afraid, you're not on your own,
the Lord is with you until he takes you home.

Rainbow

I ran towards a rainbow today,
though I could not reach its end.
It reminded me of God's promises
on which we can depend.
There'll be rain and darkness in this life,
but the sun will find its way through,
and God will shower you with his love
and shine his rainbow over you.

Light

Jesus, you are the light of the world,
we pray, let your light shine here,
we want to burn brightly for you,
so help us to draw near.
You're the fuel that feeds our flame,
there is no light without you.
Pour your oil within us, Lord,
so we can burn strong and true.
Take each vessel here and fill us up
with a never-ending supply.
Help us spread the light of you,
and fan the flames that multiply.

Sing

I sing a song of joy unto the Lord,
reflecting on his awesome majesty –
his truth, love and goodness will prevail.
He remains unchanged for eternity.
So lift up your voices and praise his name,
sing out for all you are worth,
and the angels will join you in worshipping
the creator of heaven and earth.

Change

Be prepared for change to happen,
nothing stays the same.
Life doesn't progress in an orderly fashion,
there are no rules to this game.
Be expectant and accepting,
making the best of each event,
so, hopefully, when you reflect on your life
you'll feel it was time well spent.

Call Out

Lean in to me when times are hard,
I'll see that you get through,
I know you feel you can't go on,
but I'm here to carry you.
All you see are the difficulties
and the things that hold you back
but I am here to meet your needs
and provide the things you lack.
You are my child, I love you dearly,
and I want to see you bloom.
So admit you're stuck and call out to me,
I can help if you'll give me room.

Through You

You don't need to argue my case,
you just have to act on what's true,
most people don't want clever answers
but they need to see my love in you.
So offer them comfort, help and support,
be loving and caring and kind,
then they'll see what they're missing in life,
and, through you, it's me they will find.

Tending

I weep for the loss of things that are gone,
but I can't stand still, I must move on,
walking towards a future unknown,
tending the crop of the seeds I've sown.
Choosing each path, a decision to be made,
in light of new opportunities, old ones fade.
I hope I find my destined place on earth,
and can look back with satisfaction at a life
    of worth.

Walking

Lord, help me walk in love today,
regardless of what others may say.
Help me to act how you'd want me to,
regardless of what others may do.

Fun

Help me to remember to take time out,
to have a little fun.
Help me not to always think
about things I should be getting done.
Help me to laugh at silliness,
instead of being serious all the time.
Help me to shrug off others' mistakes,
and do the same when the mistakes are
    mine.
Help me to see the special moments
that come in the everyday.
Help me to see what's really important,
so I don't miss any joy that comes my
    way.

No Fear

You love me, that's all that matters.
I need no longer fear rejection,
I'm enough as I am. I don't need to
    worry –
you aren't demanding my perfection.
You have a purpose for me,
you made me who I am.
I have in me what I need,
and you'll prepare me for your plan.

In the Gap

Lord, help me to stand in the gap
and pray with an unselfish heart.
Help me to meet the needs of others,
to be useful and play my part.
Let me not be so concerned
with myself and those closest to me.
Change me, mould me, guide me, use me,
help me become all that I should be.

Tune In

Help me hear you in the distractions,
over all the noise of the day.
Don't let me wait for peace and quiet
before I can hear what you have to say.
Help me to live in tune with you,
so that I'll always know your will,
so I'm ready to respond to your call
even in times when I'm not calm and still.

Open Heart

Lord, open my heart to the struggles of
   others,
help me to see with fresh eyes.
Many keep painful stories hidden,
so we're unaware of their bondage and ties.
Help me to look kindly on the forgotten,
help me to see their pain inside,
help me to speak of your good news to them,
so they no longer feel they must hide.

Example

I want to live a life of love,
and follow the example of Christ.
I know it won't always be easy
and I may have to pay a price.
I may face rejection, pain and taunts
as I practise what I'm called to do,
but regardless of what happens in this life
I know God's love will help me through.

Signpost

Help me to be a comfort
to those crying out in pain.
Help me to be a support
to those struggling to break each chain.
Help me to speak caring words
to those who've not heard them enough.
Help me to be a signpost
to point everyone to your love.

Flow

Lord, let your love flow out of me –
so much I can't contain.
Help me care for those in need
and minister to those in pain.
Spirit, guide me in your work,
tune my ear to hear your call,
help me see those forgotten,
the broken and forlorn.
I know that I can't do it all,
there's too much suffering,
but I can start from where I am
and share the hope you bring.
It might not look that much to others,
the small things that I do,
but I know it all adds up
when I'm obedient to you.

My All

You want me to follow you,
to listen to your call.
You don't want just part of me,
you want me to give my all.
I don't know where you'll lead me,
but I promise to follow you
and to give you all my heart
in everything I do.
I may not always get it right,
and I'm sorry if I don't,
but you've promised not to give up on me,
so I know that you won't.

Words

Lord, help me to pay proper attention,
to fully listen and not utter a word.
Let me concentrate on what's being said
so the speaker feels they've been heard.
Help me not to jump to conclusions,
to understand a different point of view.
Help me carefully consider what I might say,
and only speak words that are kind, helpful
    and true.

Draw Me In

Draw me in to your presence,
help me find release.
Let me lose myself in you,
I crave your ultimate peace.
'No more of me, but you,' I cry,
'fill me with your being.'
Transform me until it becomes
you that others are seeing.

Untidy

I'm sure that I could be really holy
if life didn't keep getting in the way –
if there was no work or commitments,
and all the mundane things to do every day.
Perhaps I should devote myself to contemplation:
become a hermit living in a cave,
not talking, or washing, just thinking deep
   thoughts.
But that's really no way I could behave.
So I guess I'll just have to manage
amid the untidiness that is everyday life,
plodding along, doing the best that I can,
and, amongst some mistakes, hope that most of
   it's right.

Replay

You forgive my mistakes,
so why do I try to hold on —
replaying silly conversations,
reliving all I've done wrong?
Help me learn, live and grow,
and find your peace at last.
Help me to put my trust in you
and let go of what's in my past.

Beat

When the world is gripping on to me
and shakes me till I'm beat,
I'll keep my eyes fixed on my Lord,
and he'll steady me on my feet.
I put my faith and trust in him —
who through the storm provides my peace.
And though my troubles won't disappear,
he'll hold me firm until they cease.

Break

Help me find some quiet
in the middle of it all.
Help me find stability
so I won't stumble, trip and fall.
Some days are lived on the edge,
with an ever-present anxiety.
There are days I want to take a break
and get away from me.

Counted

Lord, give me the courage to stand and be
   counted,
to make it known that I'm on your side,
to be able to face anything that happens,
to never deny you or run away and hide.

Think

Please give me five minutes and just let me
    be,
to sit in silence with no demands on me.
I need a moment alone to catch my breath
and think my thoughts just by myself.
I require peace and calm, so I can feel whole
to give me strength and restore my soul.

Prepare me

Prepare me, my Lord,
for the job that's in hand.
Give me wisdom and strength,
for all you have planned.
Help me remember
that it's your way that's right.
Don't let me be deceived
by those who argue and fight.
Some may lie, and plot
to turn me from my task,
but I'm obedient to you —
help me to do as you ask.
As we follow your path
some may fall away,
but those with true value
are the ones who will stay.

Willing

Who am I that God would use me?
How is it I've earned his trust?
Is it that he knows I'm willing,
and when he asks I know I must?
It's hard to fathom why he calls me
and wants me involved in his plan.
I don't think that I'm anything special,
but to God I know I am.

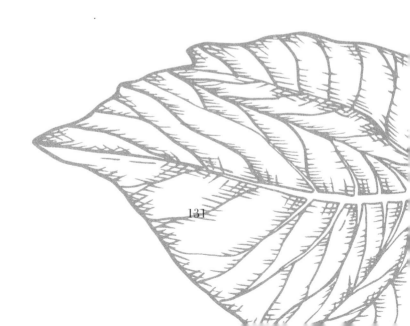

Washed

You washed away my pain and my regret,
helped me to move on and to forget.
You fill me with a joy I haven't felt before —
you've given me a peace I've always longed
     for.
You offer me a love that I could never earn,
and all you ask of me is mine in return.

Adapt

When the planning and practical things are all
    done,
when you finally stop, it's easy to feel numb —
to feel overwhelmed by the changes occurring,
by the newsfeeds, comments and rumours that
    are stirring.
But take a deep breath, stop and look around,
there is still beauty and joy and love to be
    found.
While you have to adapt and find a way
    through,
fix your thoughts on whatever is pure,
    honourable and true.

Bubble

I wish I could live in a bubble,
away from the fears of the day
in a place that is safe and controllable,
but it's impossible to exist in this way.
The world is forever changing,
and not always for the best.
I'll just have to learn to go with the flow
and trust God to deal with the rest.

Escape

Take time to discover what brings you joy
then make space for it in your life.
You need to have something to escape
    into,
a moment away from daily strife.
It's so easy just to get by each day,
working through your to-do list,
that you miss the fun and joy to be had.
Remember each day is a gift.
So find the activity that is just for you,
the time when you can let everything go.
You don't even have to be good at it,
just embrace it and go with the flow.

Retreat

I need to retreat to a world of my own,
pull up the drawbridge, pretend nobody's
  home.
There's just too much noise, my head is
  starting to spin.
There are too many demands, I can't fit it all
  in.
I need time to breathe, a chance just to stop,
to fully relax and let my whole self just flop.
I need a moment of quiet to think it all
  through,
decide what's important and what I don't need
  to do.

There are so many calls on my energy and time,
I've forgotten I can choose what I take on as
    mine.
So I'll turn off my phone and put Facebook
    away,
become much more purposeful about what I do
    in my day.
Is it truly important? Will it bring out my best?
Must I really keep rushing or can I slow down
    and rest?
I must reconnect with what's a priority to me,
but, most important of all, I need time just to
    be.

Why?

Unfortunately there is no perfect life,
so there's no point in asking "Why me?"
Everyone has their own problems,
but they don't always let you see.
Sometimes unwanted things just happen,
and often without reason,
but just remember this too shall pass,
it's all part of a season.
So try and learn to let things go
don't hold on to pain and stress,
appreciate what you have in life
and invest in your happiness.

Magic

Oh, how I wish I had a magic wand
so I could become perfect overnight.
Instead of often getting things wrong
my choices would always be right.
I want to live a life that is
a shining example to all,
instead of this constant bumbling along
where I often trip and fall.
They say that life is like a journey
and it takes time for you to grow.
But I wish my growth would hurry up,
it's happening far too slow!
But as I have no wand to wave,
I'll just have to carry on,
and at least I can find encouragement
in that it's the same for everyone.

Comments

I'm trying to learn to hold my tongue,
but it's sometimes quicker than my brain.
I make comments that I shouldn't
and afterwards feel the shame.
If all my thoughts were kind and pure,
it wouldn't matter if words did escape —
but until that time I think I'd better
seal my mouth with sticky tape.

Future

Don't fear the future that's coming,
I'll keep you firmly in my grasp.
Things will change — but don't be afraid,
I'll prepare you for all I ask.
I love you and want what's best for you,
but you won't always see my plan.
Just listen to me and I'll guide your way,
and I'll give you all that I am.

Birdsong

The sweet pure sound cuts through the noise,
causing me to stop and look for you.
I can't spot you perching within the trees
but I can hear your beautiful tune.
Your voice — so much bigger than you could
    ever be —
I wonder at your tuneful lullabies.
My attention is now on your song alone,
as I just stand and close my eyes.
It's as if your chorus was meant just for me,
sung to brighten up my day.
It makes me smile and lifts my mood –
I feel more peaceful as I go on my way.

Stir Us

Stir us up to sing your tune,
to go out and proclaim your name.
We need to share your gospel message
so people will no longer be the same.
Help us throw off our doubts and fears,
fill us up with courage inside
so that, no matter what the results,
we will always know we tried.

Printed in Great Britain
by Amazon

67497554R00088